Gladiators

Tim Collins

Badger Publishing Limited
Oldmedow Road,
Hardwick Industrial Estate,
King's Lynn PE30 4JJ
Telephone: 01438 791037

www.badgerlearning.co.uk

4 6 8 10 9 7 5

Gladiators ISBN 978-1-78147- 829-5

Text © Tim Collins 2014
Complete work © Badger Publishing Limited 2014

Publisher: Susan Ross
Senior Editor: Danny Pearson
Publishing Assistant: Claire Morgan
Designer: Fiona Grant
Series Consultant: Dee Reid

Photos: Cover image: Francesco Lacobelli/AWL Images
Page 4: © AF archive/Alamy
Page 8: © DR Travel/Alamy
Page 9: Moviestore Collection/REX
Page 10: Image Broker/REX
Page 12: Prisma/UIG/REX
Page 13: Prisma/UIG/REX
Page 14: © Image Asset Management Ltd/Alamy
Page 18: © Jon Arnold Images Ltd/Alamy
Page 20: Richard Gardner/REX
Page 21: Bebeto Matthews/AP/Press Association Images
Page 23: Prisma/UIG/REX
Page 24: Paul Cooper/REX
Page 25: Snap Stills/REX
Page 26: Jaime Abecasis/REX
Page 27: Gianluca Moggi/REX
Page 30: © Pictorial Press Ltd/Alamy

Attempts to contact all copyright holders have been made.
If any omitted would care to contact Badger Learning, we will be happy to make appropriate arrangements.

Gladiators

Contents

Vocabulary

ancient   statues

armour   survived

mosaics   tribute

opponent   trident

Sunday
XI April CL

The crowd roared as I stepped into the arena. I walked across the sand, stepping over the puddles of fresh blood.

My opponent rushed towards me, gripping his sharp dagger. It was time to fight...

1. Ancient Rome

Over 2000 years ago, the Romans were the most powerful people in the world.

They ruled over many other countries.

 The Roman Empire 2000 years ago.

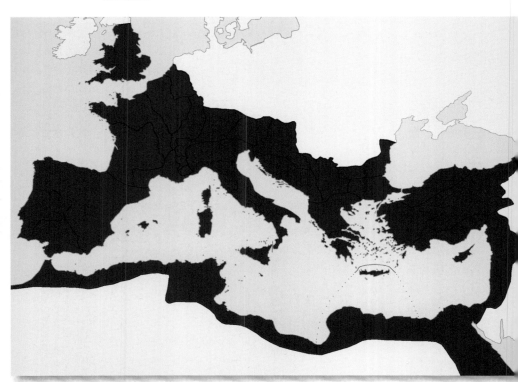

The Romans liked entertainment.

They loved to watch gladiators fight for their lives in huge arenas.

Their fights were bloody, brutal and sometimes deadly.

Romans also liked to watch chariot races on huge outdoor tracks.

They liked to bet on the races just like people bet on horse racing today.

One famous gladiator was called Spartacus. He led an army of escaped slaves but he was killed in a battle against their Roman masters.

2. Discovering the past

We know about ancient Rome because lots of books from 2000 years ago have survived.

Also many of the buildings the Romans built are still standing.

Paintings and statues can also teach us about ancient Roman life.

Many Roman buildings had wall paintings and floor mosaics. These sometimes showed pictures of gladiators fighting.

3. Gladiators

The first gladiators fought at funerals. Slaves or criminals would fight each other as a tribute to the dead person.

Romans enjoyed these fights so much they began to hold them at other times too.

At first, gladiators fought in open spaces, such as fields and marketplaces. But they proved so popular that huge arenas were built. Some arenas could hold 50,000 people.

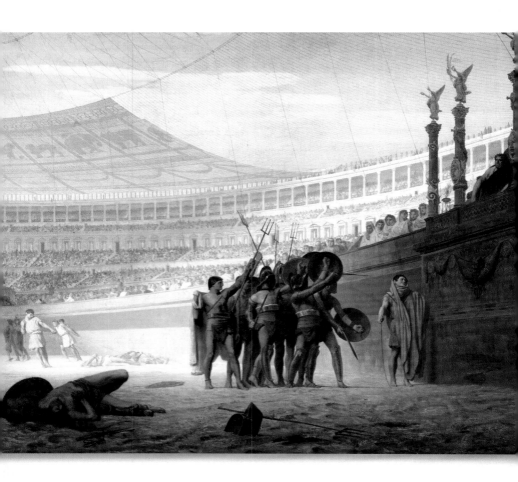

THE SOL
X SEPTEMBER CL

FLAMMA
BEATS FELIX

PLUCKY UNDERDOG
FLAMMA BEAT
FAVOURITE FELIX AT
THE ARENA YESTERDAY.
HE MOVED FASTER
THAN FELIX, LANDING
POWERFUL BLOWS
WITH HIS SWORD.

FELIX WAS SLOW,
SHOWING NONE OF
HIS USUAL ATTACKING
FORCE. HE FELL TO THE
GROUND AFTER HALF
AN HOUR AND
FLAMMA WAS DECLARED
THE WINNER.

Gladiators could become very famous
if they were good at fighting. They had
lots of fans, just like modern sports stars.

4. Deadly weapons

Different types of gladiator used different weapons. These included:

- a pair of sharp knives
- a trident and a net
- a sword and shield
- a bow and arrow
- a spear and a suit of armour

Which do you think would have been the most deadly?

Not all gladiators were men. Some women fought too. But lots of people thought this was wrong, and female gladiators were eventually banned.

Sometimes crowds in arenas would start rioting. A riot in the town of Pompeii killed hundreds, and led to a ban on gladiator shows for ten years.

5. Battle in the arena

Some people think gladiators always fought to the death, but most of the time they did not.

Gladiators were highly trained fighters, and it would be a waste of time and money if they only lasted for one contest.

Gladiators were usually slaves or criminals, but some were volunteers.

Why would someone risk their life in the arena?

If you were a popular gladiator you could become very rich and famous. Even as a slave you could sometimes win your freedom.

Arena shows could be very grand. Sometimes the entire floor was flooded and sea battles were acted out.

WOW! facts

The biggest sporting venue in ancient Rome was the Circus Maximus. It could hold a quarter of a million people. That's more than the stadiums of Manchester City, Manchester United, Liverpool and Arsenal put together.

These shows were very expensive, so who paid for them?
It was the politicians. They thought the public would be
more likely to vote for them if they gave them amazing
entertainment.

6. Gory entertainment

Gladiators were just part of the gory entertainment in ancient Rome.

There were also beast shows where animals such as lions were put in the arena with people.

Criminals would be thrown to these beasts without any weapons to defend themselves. They would suffer painful, gory deaths in front of the cheering crowds.

Some criminals were so scared of facing the animals that they would try to kill themselves before they went in, so guards watched over them.

Sometimes criminals were even murdered in the theatre. They would take the place of one of the actors at the end of a play and be killed for real.

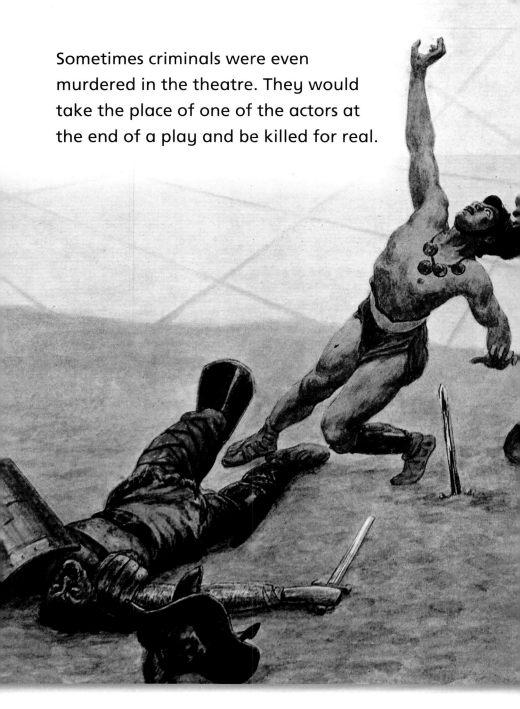

A Roman emperor called Commodus shocked crowds by taking part in gladiatorial battles himself. He is a major character in the film *Gladiator*.

Sunday
Xl April CL

My opponent tumbled to the sand, clutching the gash in his stomach. I lifted my bloody sword into the air and the crowd cheered...

I turned to the emperor. He stood up and looked at the crowd. They were cheering wildly and waving their arms. He gave me the order. I swiftly cut off my opponent's head...

WOW! facts

The crowd played a big part in deciding if a defeated gladiator should be killed by his opponent. They would shout and signal with their hands. Nobody wanted to anger the mob!

Questions

How do we know so much about ancient Rome?
(page 10)

Where did the first gladiator fights take place? *(page 12)*

Name three weapons used by gladiators. *(page 17)*

Who were gladiators? *(page 21)*

Who paid for the gladiator shows? *(page 23)*

Why do you think we don't have gladiators today?

Index